DYNAMIC SMALL GROUPS

DYNAMIC SMALL GROUPS

A COMMUNITY OF FRIENDS

RICK THOMAS

DYNAMIC SMALL GROUPS:
A Community of Friends

ISBN 978-1-966741-16-9

Rick Thomas

Edited by Sheron Wallace

Life Over Coffee
8595 Pelham Rd Ste 400 #406,
Greenville, SC 29615
LifeOverCoffee.com

Dedication

To the faithful small group leaders—
You are the "pastors on the ground," the shepherds
tending the flock in the everyday moments of life.
Your work is not simply facilitating meetings; you are
discipling souls, bearing burdens, speaking truth, and
modeling Christlike love. Your effort is the heavy lifting
of ministry—work that often goes unseen, yet carries
eternal value.

Your labor strengthens the church, lightens the load
of your pastors, and advances the kingdom in ways
only heaven will fully reveal. Every conversation, every
prayer, every moment spent pointing others to Christ
is an investment in eternity.

May this book serve as both a tool and an
encouragement as you continue the sacred work of
making disciples. Press on with your watering and
planting, knowing that your toil for the Lord is never in
vain (1 Corinthians 15:58).

For additional resources, visit
lifeovercoffee.com

Table of Contents

Introduction 8

1 Budgeting Sin.. 14

2 Let's Have a Conflict 22

3 A Bible or Mentor? 30

4 Cure for Shallow Groups... 38

5 Three Dynamic Keys 48

6 Loving the Difficult 56

7 Let's Get Practical.. 62

8 A Guide for Leaders.. 70

Conclusion 80

About the Author 83

Introduction

Being part of a small group can be a rewarding experience, or it can be the most challenging part of your week. A thriving small group doesn't happen by accident—it requires clear direction, purposeful engagement, and intentional equipping. Each member plays a role, but without a well-thought-out plan, the group may struggle.

As you start this book, I want to help you assess your small group experience. Whether you lead a group or simply participate, this eight point diagnostic will provide insight into where your group stands. If you've never been in a small group or are considering joining or starting one, these principles will guide you. I'll walk you through eight essential components of a robust small group, each with a brief explanation and a question for reflection. I encourage you to discuss your responses with a friend, reinforcing these principles in both your life and your group.

1—*What is your group's purpose?* Is it a Bible study? If so, study the Bible. If its purpose is to transform lives, make sure everyone knows it's a sanctification group. For this book, I'm working under the assumption that the purpose of your small group is the biblical transformation of the members in the group—what I'm calling a sanctification group.

QUESTION: What is the purpose of your group? Does everyone know the purpose of your group? If it is a sanctification group, there are three ways to measure this:

- They come prepared to change themselves.
- The conversation is about how each person can change.
- Your post-meeting connections during the week continue the process of change.

2—*Learn to share incrementally.* Most participants in a sanctification group are insecure about sharing the details of their lives. Openly sharing is not a call to blurt out the worst facts about yourself the first night you're in the group, but if you want to change, you must be willing to reveal more and more of yourself to the other members.

QUESTION: Is your group an environment of grace that makes sharing your life with others compelling? Are you holding back from sharing the story God is writing in your life? If so, why are you doing so?

3—*You need the Bible, plus.* Don't fall into the trap that says the Bible is all you need to change. If the Bible were all you needed, the Ethiopian would not have been perplexed in Acts 8 as he was reading his Bible. If the Bible is all you need, there would be no need for teachers of the Bible. If the Bible were all you needed, there would not be all the "one another" commands in the New Testament. The issue here is not about minimizing God's Word but maximizing the community of faith that is called to come alongside each other to help work the Word of God deep into one another's souls.

QUESTION: Do you know how to bring the Bible to bear on your most recurring sin problem? Do you know how to walk a member of your small group through their recurring struggle?

4—*Application of the gospel requires effort.* We tend to be lazy when it comes to messy, hardcore sanctification problems. It's easier to read the Bible in a silo than work it out in a community, i.e., marriage and family. Burden bearing is not a job for the lazy person.

QUESTION: Are you genuinely interested in the struggles of those in your small group? Hebrews 10:24-25 talks about considering one another. How do you consider those in your group?

5—*Sanctification is dangerous.* Once you open the sanctification can of worms in an individual's life, all bets are off. Your relationship can go to some challenging places, which is why people are tempted to bury their noses in the Bible, hoping the moment of transparency passes them by. It's less dangerous than opening your heart about a recurring struggle. It is even possible to use the Bible (or any other book) to hide in plain sight of your small group. However, intentional biblical sanctification is a wholly different matter that is intrusive and life-changing.

QUESTION: Do you use anything as a shield to keep from revealing your true self to others? The Bible? Other books? Too much talking? A quietness that dares others to approach you? Do you keep the conversation shallow?

6—*Don't fall into the nugget-ology trap.* We can minimize God's work in our lives when we talk about "what God taught me today." What if that is not the whole truth about our week? We can hide our sanctification garbage under the nugget of the day—the meme we read on social media or heard during the Sunday sermon.

QUESTION: Is the motive of what you share in the group to reveal more and more of yourself because you want others to know you so they can come alongside you to help you change?

7—*Ignorance may play a role.* Stated simply, we don't know any better. "This is how we've always done it." The gospel never changes, but we must change, or our religion will go stale. Progressive sanctification is progressive transformation. Christ wants us to learn the Bible facts and then learn how to apply those facts to our lives practically. This means as we grow, we will change our understanding and practice. We cannot become stale like the Pharisees, who disdained change. If you want to be in a safe place, you might work hard to keep from changing. True refuge (safety) is in Christ and His body, where we're all knitted together, nourished by Him, and nourishing one another for His fame and our maturity.

QUESTION: How is the practical gospel transforming you and your relationships? The gospelized person has nothing to protect, nothing to hide, and nothing to fear. For freedom, He has set us free (Galatians 5:1).

8—*Refrain from the magic Bible approach.* "If you just read it, you will change." While that is true—to a degree—it is not true if you want sustained and comprehensive change. Yes, there is passive obedience (sit and soak), but there is active obedience, too: be doers of the Word; work out what God is working in you. The mystical approach may make you feel better because you shared some Bible facts with a friend, but that does not change you in all the ways you could change.

QUESTION: What does active obedience look like in your small group, particularly how you are actively engaging your friends at the core of their souls?

Call to Action

No matter your role in a small group, will you take the time to answer these questions?

1. If you are a leader, will you share what insights you gained with the person overseeing you? Take the opportunity to evaluate your group's maturity, identify areas for growth, and establish a clear, actionable plan for change.
2. If you are a member, will you discuss this content with your small group leader? Consider how you can contribute to the group's growth by assessing its current state and what steps are necessary for meaningful progress to deeper maturity.
3. Leaders, I encourage you to introduce these essentials to your group, fostering open discussions, appealing to them to become part of your group's sanctification rhythm.

I hope that as you read on, your understanding and practice of small group dynamics will deepen, and your conversations will become richer. We were never meant to grow alone—sanctification happens in a community. May this book be a resource you return to often as you pursue a thriving, Christ-centered small group.

Rick

1

Budgeting Sin

The title sounds careless and possibly scary, but before you blow a gasket, let me ask, "Have you reached sinless perfection yet?" We can pretend there is a secret in our lives, but the truth is that it is not a secret at all: we still sin against God and each other. We might love God and others as we love ourselves, but we most certainly sin against God and others, too. This undeniable truth is a call to action to prepare for the inevitable. Like a wise financial steward who knows hard times are coming, he budgets for those difficult days.

An Uncertain Sound

Someone once said, "One can acquire anything in solitude except character." The scriptures clearly recognize this sentiment. Throughout the New Testament, sanctification happens more in corporate contexts than in isolation. Paul wrote mostly to New Testament churches, teaching these local communities how to live well together. According to Paul's theology, individuals were an essential means of grace in helping others grow into Christian maturity. The primary roadblock to personal growth and relational harmony is sin: sin in our own lives, sin in others, and sin in a fallen world.

Do you remember the first time you heard yourself on an audio recording? Were you surprised at how you sounded? Guess what: no one else was surprised. Everyone in the room—except for you—knew how you sounded. You were the last to know what everyone else already knew. As this experience demonstrates, the value of people's input into your life cannot be over-estimated. One of the many kindnesses of God is that He gives us people who are willing to help us grow closer to Him.

- God gives us friends to help reveal our sins to us.
- God gives us friends to help us deal with our sins.
- God gives us friends to encourage us as we plod through this fallen world.
- God gives us friends to help them the same way they are helping us.

A rich man is a person who has mature Christian friends who are willing and able to help him grow into spiritual manhood. A wise man is a man who makes it easy for his friends to care for him by insisting that they be honest in their assessments. Ken Sande confronts the foolish man's selfish responses to this kind of care in this passage from his book, *The Peacemaker*:

> The Bible teaches that we should see conflict neither as an inconvenience nor as an occasion for selfish gain but rather as an opportunity to demonstrate God's presence and power. It encourages us to look at conflict as an opportunity to glorify God, serve others, and grow to be like Christ.

Embrace Conflict

Like death and taxes, sin is inevitable. We are fallen people living in a fallen world. Sin happens to all of us. The sad truth is not so much that sin happens; we understand why sin happens. The unfortunate truth is that most Christians are ill-equipped to respond godly to the sin that does happen. Reflect on these biblical teachings on sin:

> And he said to his disciples, "Temptations to sin are sure to come."
>
> (Luke 17:1)

> Therefore, confess your sins to one another and pray for one another that you may be healed.
>
> (James 5:16)

> If we (Christians) say we (Christians) have no sin, we deceive ourselves, and the truth is not in us.
>
> (1 John 1:8)

> Brothers, if anyone is caught in any [sin], you who are spiritual should restore him in a spirit of gentleness. Keep watch on yourself, lest you too be tempted [to sin].
>
> (Galatians 6:1)

If sin is sure to come, small groups provide fantastic contexts for the people in a local church to apply the gospel to their sins.

All In the Family

We see our family in a similar way to small group life. The point of our parenting was not to stop our children from sinning. That would be a frustrating and impossible task. Our goal was to provide a context for our kids to succeed and fail and to respond godly to both inevitabilities. We wanted to encourage, motivate, and celebrate with them when they succeeded, and we tried to comfort, confront, and encourage them when they sinned. What better place for our kids to sin than in our family, where we can equip them for a better life? Similarly, a small group is a great family context for success and failure. A strong small group embraces the positive and negative of people's lives while coming alongside their members to equip them for life.

Embracing Conflict

- **THE BAD NEWS:** We are sinners who live and sin alongside other sinners in a fallen world.
- **THE GOOD NEWS:** The gospel is the perfect solution for sinners who sin in a fallen world.

I realize it will not surprise most of you to hear this, but I will say it anyway: we are not in heaven yet! The obvious implication is that when God saved you—assuming you are a Christian—you were not sanctified entirely. You have not reached perfection. From a Christian worldview, we understand complete sanctification to happen only when we reach heaven. The sobering reality for all of us is that the time between God saving us and God bringing us to our eternal home is a progressively sanctified kind of life. With that in mind, there are at least two ways we can respond to the doctrine of sin as it intersects with the doctrine of man.

- We can deny that sin exists in our lives.
- We can embrace this sobering reality by aggressively fighting sin in the context of friends who are trying to do the same for the glory of God.

Deniers, Avoiders, and the Fearful

Have you ever heard that the gospel is for our salvation and the gospel is for our sanctification? I firmly believe this statement is true and would further assert that any Christian who wants to live wonderfully and victoriously in this life must embrace it. However, when I or anyone else says the gospel is for our salvation and the gospel is for our sanctification, there is an unspoken and undeniable implication that sin is involved in some way. The gospel always implies that sin is present. If there was no sin, there would be no need for the gospel. The introduction of the gospel (Christ) came after sin entered the world (Genesis 3:15). If Adam had not fallen in the Garden of Eden, he (and we) would not need a Redeemer.

But we do need a Redeemer, and He (Christ) implies sin, and sin implies Him (the gospel). Most people understand and readily accept this truth when it comes to salvation. They know they need salvation from their sin, but where the rub comes into play is how we think and live between the time God regenerated us and the time He takes us to heaven. My response to this concern is revealed in the statement, "The gospel saves us (redemption), and the gospel sustains us (sanctification)." We never come to a place in our lives, pre- or post-salvation, where we do not need the gospel. We need the gospel to fight sin! Whether someone needs to be saved or sustained, they need the gospel. Over the years, I have run into three general categories of people who struggle with the "sin is present with us" concept.

THE DENIERS: This group of sincere Christians says that sin does not exist once you become a Christian. They say, "I am dead to sin." This concept is a gross misinterpretation of Scripture and is a product of legalism. Legalists try very hard to separate themselves from sin, even to the point of denying it.

> Do not love the world or the things in the world. If anyone loves the world, the love of the Father is not in him. For all that is in the world—the desires of the flesh and the desires of the eyes and pride of life—is not from the Father but is from the world.
> (1 John 2:15-16)

They misinterpret John's understanding of worldliness by teaching that worldliness is in the world as opposed to being in the person. John placed worldliness in the heart. For the deniers to be true to their theology, they have to ignore, re-categorize, or justify their sins. These options are untenable because they lead to personal frustration, self-deception, and relational conflict. Eventually, they can harden their hearts such that their sin is imperceptible to them.

THE AVOIDERS: This group puts their fingers in their ears and screams, "Na-Na-Na-Na-Na-Na-Na-Na-Na-" ad infinitum. They are sincere and want to live for Christ, just like the deniers want to live for Christ. Sadly, they are stricken with the same—dare I say it—sin. "If you say you have no sin, you make God a liar, and the truth is not in you." Those are John's words to Christians in 1 John 1:8, not mine. To be an avoider, you have to recategorize, ignore, and rationalize your sins. Avoiders go from conflict to conflict, rarely ever resolving the trouble in their lives or relationships.

THE FEARFUL: This group knows they sin, but they try hard to ignore it because they don't want to be found out. Transparency is a frightening proposition for them. To be open and honest about their most personal struggles is not a best-case scenario for the insecure. This posture toward their sin is self-righteousness, as they present an artificial righteousness that does not belong to Christ. Many times, these people come from dysfunctional and critical familial relationships. For example, they may have had harsh dads, or they were part of a legalistic religious culture. They hear about the grace of God and His lack of judgment, but overreact by denying the truthfulness of their sinfulness. They honestly can't juxtapose sin and grace the way Paul did. (See 1 Timothy 1:15-16).

Ignoring Sin Neutralizes the Gospel

To avoid, deny, or respond fearfully to the real and objective sin in our post-salvation experience is to mock and devalue the gospel. To say we have no sin is to say we do not need the gospel. This anti-gospel worldview is a dangerous and heretical position for any believer (or unbeliever) to take. If the unbeliever or believer rejected the truth about sin as though they did not believe in its reality, there would be no need for the gospel. Jesus did not come for the healthy. He came for sick people, which brings us to the value and efficacy of small groups for those who are willing to deal with their sins. Sanctification is a community event, a shared life between fellow sinners who God's grace has saved. A small group that embraces the reality of sin and the potential conflict it brings will position itself to resolve its conflicts in ways that glorify God and transforms the members of the group.

Call to Action

1. Do you sin? This is not a trick question.
2. Do you believe you need others to help you walk through your sin?
3. Do you believe others need you so you can help them walk through their sin?
4. If you answered "yes" to my questions, how are you setting the example by personally confessing your sins to others and letting others know and experience your care for them when they sin? See 1 John 1:9; James 5:16.

2

Let's Have a Conflict

Sometimes in life, you have to get into a conflict with someone. This dreaded reality is not a wish, desire, or prayer request but rather a common-sense perspective that comes with living in a sin-cursed world. It is impossible to have two or more humans living close to each other for an extended period and not have relational conflict. Sin does not accommodate our desires for peace or present a path of least resistance. Dealing with reality is a better starting point than pretending that bad things will never happen.

You Must Try

Sin is divisive and will do all it can to bring relational confusion and frustration between two people. This aim of sin is not discouraging for the gospel-minded individual because we are not people without hope (1 Corinthians 15:19). We live in the transformational reality and hoped-filled expectation of the gospel. The divisiveness of sin does not have the ultimate power over us (Romans 6:14). We are more than conquerors because of Christ's work on our behalf (Romans 8:31-39). Thus, when conflict happens, we have choices. There are two primary ways to avoid tension with another person. We can choose to live superficially with them, or we can choose not to reconcile with them after disagreements happen.

Either course of action is not tenable for the Christian. We are not allowed to live superficial lives with others or allowed to ignore gospel-reconciling opportunities. God calls us to pursue each other in gospel transformation for His glory and our personal and communal benefit. To not be active in stirring others up in love and good deeds is a betrayal of the gospel call on our lives (Hebrews 10:24-25). Imagine being part of a group of friends that does not seek to pursue each other to motivate each other toward life change. Superficial friend groups are a mockery of the gospel. It's like going to the hospital while refusing to access the hospital's resources—a means of grace that has the possibility of radically changing your life.

Prancing Elephants

One of our Adamic tendencies is to avoid the obvious flaws we see in each other. Perhaps you have done this. I have. You're in a situation, and you perceive relational awkwardness in one of your friends. At that moment, you have to make a choice: will I begin to pray about a strategy to pursue this person for their good and God's glory, or will I ignore the big fat elephant that just went prancing across the room—right in front of me? One of your temptations will be to avoid the big fat elephant in the room because you know the possibility of a relational tussle happening if you pursue the person to help them.

A dispute will probably ensue if you pursue the person because two things are working against you: you will seek your friend imperfectly, and your friend will receive your care imperfectly. Therefore, you have to decide. Do you want to love this person even though there will probably be a season of relational dysfunction, or do you want to ignore the God opportunity in front of you? The Christian who wants to live for God's glory will not have the heart to walk away from this opportunity that his Commander and Chief has placed in front of him. It would be like being on a battlefield and ignoring the general's command to engage the enemy. (The enemy is not your friend but is the spiritual warfare you're engaged in on behalf of your friend.)

Conflict like Jesus

My dear friends, we are living on a battlefield, and the enemy is amongst us. He is alive and well on planet Earth, and he will be in our hearts until our great Commander comes to take us home. Until then, the battle will never slacken. We cannot avoid the obvious things in our lives and relationships. If we ignore our relational tensions, it is not loving, but it is self-centered laziness born out of our desire for personal comfort and reputation. I understand the tension and temptation. It would be hypocritical for me to slack away from God's call on my life to press into my sanctification while seeking to help others in theirs.

This kind of gospel-motivated presupposition implies life will be hard, but we must not flinch. This mindset is how Jesus lived. He went from one relational conflict to another. Every encounter had the potential to turn into a conflict. This perspective is evident in His encounters with the Pharisees and among His close friends. At the end of His life, the disciples' frustration level was so high that they denied being His friends (Matthew 26:74). However, Christ was a Johnny-one-note kind of guy: He did not hide how He thought about living for God. Though He was loving, He was also clear—if you're going to follow Him, you must prepare to die (Mark 10:22; Luke 14:26).

Choose to Pursue

We live in an imperfect world, and we are imperfect people. To expect relationships to go smoothly is to live in an illusion. It's like a man wearing a white suit in the desert, hoping never to get dirty. Though you don't have a "fight wish," you must know that you cannot go on for any length of time with your friends and not have relational conflicts. If you're married, think about how impossible it is to live perfectly with your spouse to where you are not sinning against them, and they are not sinning against you, which brings me to my second point.

- **POINT TWO:** You can choose not to reconcile after disagreements happen.

My first point was about whether you're going to choose superficial friends or biblical friends. If you choose biblical friends, then batten down the hatches because you're going to get up into each other's business, and you're going to get your feelings hurt. You will sin against them while you try to go deeper into those relationships. And they will sin against you. It is unavoidable. My second point is whether you will choose to reconcile after a breach happens in the relationship. Paul said it this way:

> Live in harmony with one another. Do not be haughty, but associate with the lowly. Never be wise in your own sight. Repay no one evil for evil, but give thought to do what is honorable in the sight of all. If possible, so far as it depends on you, live peaceably with all. Beloved, never avenge yourselves, but leave it to the wrath of God, for it is written, "Vengeance is mine, I will repay, says the Lord." To the contrary, "If your enemy is hungry, feed him; if he is thirsty, give him something to drink; for by so doing you

will heap burning coals on his head." Do not be
overcome by evil, but overcome evil with good.
(Romans 12:16-21)

What Depends on You?

The Romans passage gives us a clear and distinct advantage
over our friends who reject Christ. We can do what they
can't—we can reconcile. The issue is not and should never
be, "Will we get into an argument?" It should always be, "Will
we reconcile after we get into an inevitable argument?" As
Paul implied, there is a conditionality to reconciliation—so
far as it depends on you, live peaceably with all. Sadly, some
people will not want to reconcile. What the other person
did should not be your first point of focus. You never want
to start with what they did or what they are currently doing
(Matthew 7:3-5). I hear this when I talk to people about
broken relationships. A person will begin talking about
what the other party did and how it hurt them. There is a
place for that conversation, but the bulk of Paul's words are
for us, not the other person (Romans 12:16-21).

- How are you overcoming evil with good?
- Do you have a desire to reconcile with the other
  person?
- What is your plan (your strategy) for reconciliation?
- What is the content of your prayers regarding your
  heart and the other person?
- How are you asking the Father to bring
  reconciliation?

I Don't Like You

Recently, someone said, "She does not like me anymore and won't have anything to do with me." The lady who said this was a believer, and she was talking about another believer. My soul was sad. How can it be? How can a Christian carry a grudge or rotten attitude toward another Christian for an indefinite period and not seek to repair the relationship? This posture is gospel insanity. How can a Christian say to another Christian, "I do not like you anymore?" Really. Is this possible? What is going on in our hearts when we hold onto our hurts indefinitely while not living in the immeasurable grace the Father provides?

I know quarrels happen, but where I struggle is when there is no plan for reconciliation. One of the most defaming things a Christian can do to their Savior is to allow conflict to continue between two people. It's a clear sign of gospel dysfunction of the heart, either from one or both people in the battle. We have the power of God resident within us. Still, we will allow ourselves to succumb to the power of evil to the point where the evil can so overcome us that we permanently dismiss each other. You may never reconcile with someone, but you can do as much as depends on you, and you do not have to carry the hurt in your heart to where you become a captured victim.

Your Best Friends

Your best friends will be those who were previously separated from you by sin. It happened two ways: you sinned against them, and they sinned against you. The mature Christian does not focus on who fired the first shot. Neither of you was looking for a fight, but it happened. Boom! You are in a conflict with someone. Though the rupture in the relationship matters, the bigger issue is the gospel and how you both will apply it to your lives. Will you activate the power of the gospel in your life? Perhaps only one will, and if that is the case, it must be you. But if both do, you will reconcile, and more than likely, you'll become friends for life.

Once you go to the mat with someone and get back up as friends, nothing is left to hide or defend. You have seen the worst in each other, but you decided the gospel will have more power over your relationship than the disruption. The gospel can do this for friendships. It can take the inevitable fight and transform the combatants into the best of friends. The people who have my back are those I have sinned against, and they forgave me. They are the people I want to have my back because I know their love for me is genuine. Perhaps there are folks in your life who refuse to reconcile with you. Let me give you two parting pieces of advice. One is from a friend who helped me many years ago, and the other is from Paul.

- **YOUR MINDSET:** "I can't make you love me, but you can't stop me from loving you."
- **PAUL'S MINDSET:** "Do not be overcome by evil, but overcome evil with good."

Call to Action

Many folks reading this will focus on that relationship that remains fractured. The disappointment can weigh heavy on you. I understand. My appeal is for you to ask the Lord to provide a restful heart despite any challenging relationship you might have. As you are working to rest, ask Him what you can do—if anything—to fulfill what Paul said about "as much as it depends on you."

1. Describe a time when you got into a conflict with someone and reconciled. What were a few things you learned about God and yourself during that awkward season?
2. Describe a relationship that remains fractured. Have you done everything that is dependent on you? If not, what do you need to do? Will you run this by a friend to gain their perspective?
3. If you have done all that you should, are you resting in the Lord's grace? The way to know if you are is by how you talk about that person. If you're critical or unkind in your speech, you have some heart work to do, and you have yet to do all that depends upon you.

3

A Bible or Mentor?

Would it be better to have a Bible or a mentor? You might think this is a trick question, though it is not meant to be. The potential dilemma is intended to provoke you to think first, respond second, and discuss thoroughly. The obvious answer to the question is both. The Bible does not say the Bible alone is all you need to change. The Bible does not suggest that all you need is a discipler. At different times and in different ways, the Bible makes a case for both of these options to be part of a person's overall soul care package. Actually, the Bible teaches that there are five ways a person can change.

Five Ways

- The Lord will change you (Ephesians 2:8).
- The Bible will change you (2 Timothy 3:16).
- You must do something to change (Philippians 2:12).
- Other people will help you to change (2 Samuel 12:1).
- Situations will change you (Genesis 50:20).

All five ways should be part of any Christian's change process. The neglect of any one of them will hinder a person's maturation-into-Christlikeness process. My point is not about how one is better than the other but about how all of them are essential, and each one serves a unique role in the overall transformation of any person. It is similar to Paul's discussion about the different gifts within the body of Christ (1 Corinthians 12:12-26). All the parts of the body are needed, and it is not helpful to speak more of one to the neglect of the other. It depends on the need of the moment and the specific situation a person is going through, which determines how we use each component of the change process.

There is a time when the Bible should be front and center in a person's life, and there is a time when a person needs to put the Bible down and do the hard work of repenting (changing). I do not need the Bible to repent if the Bible has already taught me how to repent. For example, when I get angry at my wife, I do not need the Bible to explain my anger, what is going on in my heart, or what I need to do about my sin. The Bible has already informed me about these things. I need to confess my sins to God and my wife and seek their forgiveness (1 John 1:9). At that moment of conviction, the most important thing that I need to do is number three—personal responsibility in the Bible's change process. God's Word had already done its job. The Spirit was doing His job. My call to action during any bout of anger is to repent. Will I step up to the plate and do what I need to do to mature in Christ?

It's Both And

Back to my question: what is better to have, the Bible or a mentor? You see this biblical synchronization between the essentialness of the Bible and a mentor in the New Testament. Here are a few examples:

> Go therefore and make disciples of all nations, baptizing them in the name of the Father and of the Son and of the Holy Spirit, teaching them to observe all that I have commanded you. And behold, I am with you always, to the end of the age.
> (Matthew 28:19-20)

> But how are they to call on him in whom they have not believed? And how are they to believe in him of whom they have never heard? And how are they to hear without someone preaching? And how are they to preach unless they are sent? As it is written, "How beautiful are the feet of those who preach the good news!"
>
> (Romans 10:14-15)

> So Philip ran to him and heard him reading Isaiah the prophet and asked, "Do you understand what you are reading?" And he said, "How can I unless someone guides me?" And he invited Philip to come up and sit with him.
>
> (Acts 8:30-31)

For more examples of the primacy of the community of humanity mentoring each other, read all the "one another" passages from the New Testament. The Bible does not make a case for Bible exclusivity in the sanctification process but calls for a more comprehensive way to think about our sanctification, which requires a healthy (biblical) view of the Bible as well as how we engage each other (koinonia). Christians do not separate sola Scripture from mentoring or the other three essential elements in the change process: the Lord, the person, and the situation. Every Timothy needs a Paul, plus a thorough understanding of the Lord's Word.

Community Contexts

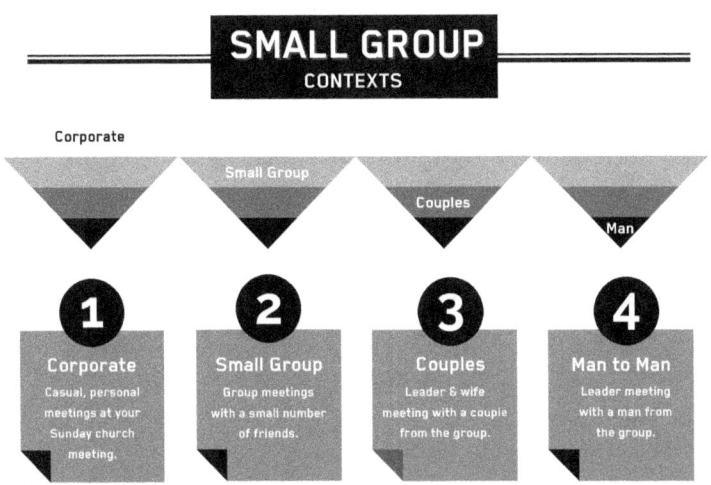

Discipleship, working in cooperation with growing Bible knowledge, while in the context of a community, is an excellent prescription for anyone to mature in Christ. This perspective is the way I have always led small groups in the local church. If you have a high view of the Word of God and a high view of the community, you do not need convincing about how they work together in the overall transformation of souls. For example, this worldview for small group development works well in four local church contexts.

1. Corporate meetings
2. Small group meetings
3. Couple meetings
4. Personal meetings

Corporate Meetings

Many local churches have one big church meeting each week. It happens on Sunday morning. This corporate event is a time when everyone comes together as a larger body to worship the Lord through singing, hearing the Word, ministering to each other, and eclectic teaching contexts. These opportunities are specific events that work together to build up the body collectively. Typically, the corporate meeting is an excellent time for the small group to connect, even if it is a lighthearted moment. You may joke around, catch up on your week, and possibly talk about something serious. Due to the frenetic pace of the morning, these pneumatic opportunities are not always conducive to deep and transformative conversations.

They are brief encounters, albeit redemptive, in that, you see each other, and it is another opportunity to build relationally, with the long-term goal and expectation of having more in-depth and more transformative times later. The deeper discussions of life cannot happen consistently in a large crowd of people with whom you do not do life together regularly. To expect the large corporate church meeting to be a context for more in-depth and uniquely personal transformative conversations could be a setup for disappointment. You need another place that provides more privacy, with a slower pace, to talk about the more profound things in our lives. This need and opportunity is why some churches have small groups.

Small Group Meetings

The groups that I have led typically met on Sunday or Wednesday nights throughout the year. We gathered to take our relationships deeper than what we could do on Sunday mornings. These meetings were more isolated and private from the larger corporate body. The nature of these smaller meetings gave us better opportunities to be more honest and transparent. Our "rule" in a small group is that what we say in this room stays in this room. Our small groups were a tight-knit group of friends who came together to spur each other on to love and good works (Hebrews 10:24-25).

Small group meetings are a time for the pace and noise of our lives to slow down. It is the "pulling away" idea that the Lord taught His disciples (Mark 6:30-32). There are times when it is essential to get away from serving others so that you can help yourself. Without a replenishing context in your life, you will quickly deplete your soul. This kind of context is essential for individuals, couples, and families. It is a quiet, private, smaller corporate time where members can humbly ask each other to speak into their lives. It presumes self-acknowledgment of self-suspicion. We have our blind spots, which elevates the value of a band of brothers and sisters reciprocally caring for each other.

Couple's Meetings

Because of our sense of shame, the temptation to be easily embarrassed, and a lack of community trust, we have found that adding monthly couple's meetings to our small group dynamic is a must. The curse of Adam not only reaches far and wide, but it goes deep, too. Love, trust, and safety do not happen just because you are Christians and you are meeting in a small group. Some people are more jaded about opening up in a small group because of past experiences where others have hurt them. Besides, some conversations are not suitable for small group life.

We do not talk about a couple's sex life in our small group meetings. This discussion is where the couple's sessions can serve as an essential means of grace for a struggling marriage. It gives them a safer and smaller place to talk about things that are important to them. Couples meetings can also be dynamic when all the members of the small group value and participate in them. Couples sessions are not just for the leader to care for the group but an opportunity for the entire group to meet in small contexts so they can learn to love and serve each other.

Private Meetings

As you can see, our meetings go from broad to narrow. Our most non-transparent meetings are the corporate meetings on Sunday mornings because those meetings cannot accommodate the more in-depth sanctification care of the smaller group contexts. Corporate meetings are essential and fantastic for other things, i.e., corporate teaching, worship, training, and prayer. Even our small group meetings are not enough for us to do sanctification well because there are too many people in the room to talk about the more intimate and vulnerable things in our lives.

Some of the most effective envisioning and equipping in our small groups happened when the individuals and couples in the group were meeting privately with the leader and each other. For the group to be a success, all the members must pursue one another. Each person in the group will have to decide if they are going to own their group. The degree to which each person takes ownership of their group will determine the quality of sanctification that happens in the group. If the couples and individuals are meeting in various contexts throughout the week, the small group meeting can be transformational. However, if the group is not getting to know each other on more individual levels, the group meeting may indeed be smaller than the corporate meeting, but it will still be a group of superficial strangers.

Call to Action

What is better to have, a Bible or a mentor? It is better to have both plus the other three elements of change the Bible speaks of. It is like a church with a pro-life emphasis, adoption ministry, global outreach, and Bible studies. It is not that one is better, to the exclusion of the others. They are all essential. When it comes to sanctification, it is better to think and implement broadly rather than narrowly. As you think about your sanctification, is there a missing element?

1. Are you mature in the Bible but weak in transparent relationships?
2. Do you know what to do but are unwilling to be personally responsible or vulnerable to change?
3. Are you lovingly intrusive in the lives of those in your sphere of influence?
4. What do you need to do to access all the means of grace the Lord provides for you and your friends to change?

4

Cure for Shallow Groups

Is your small group living in-depth, transparent, intentional, reciprocating lives who have strong desires to change personally and as a group? Perhaps it's a men's group or a community group of ladies. It could be a mixed group that meets to go over the sermon or a book. How would you describe those gatherings? One of the most significant pitfalls that can stagnate any small group of believers is shallowness, which implies they have no transformative force in the individual lives and there is a growing frustration among some participants due to the general shallowness of the group.

My Group Won't Get Real

Consider Biff, a regular small group attendee. Biff asked his group's leader if they could meet for breakfast. He wanted to share a complaint about their little group. Biff believed the group was not progressing toward an objective meaningful goal, and, from his perspective, he knew why. The following week, they met, and Biff shared several illustrations about how the group seemed stuck in what he called a superficial mode. He said no one demonstrated any interest in getting real. Biff's complaint is one of the more common ones that I hear about small group life. Here are a few grievances I have heard, which is not an exhaustive list. If you belong to a small group that wants to go deeper while maturing in Christ, it would be an excellent opportunity to discuss these common complaints. Perhaps you might want to add others to my list.

"We meet to go through a book or watch a video, but nobody says anything. I keep my mouth shut, too, and leave frustrated."

"My husband and I have been struggling for years, but there is no way I would say anything in our group. We'd be the only ones with problems."

"It's a lack of transparency if you ask me. These people are not about being open."

"I would say something, but if they knew what was going on in my heart, they wouldn't want to be around me."

"I shared one time when I was struggling through something, and the group gave me a few cliches. Then, they shared some scriptures that did not help. I was embarrassed for weeks after sharing. I learned from that experience to keep my mouth shut about things that mattered."

"I would share, but my small group leader has more problems than I do."

"I'm not sure that my leader can help me. He's a facilitator more than a leader. He wants to stick to the script that the pastor gives him. When folks have tried to share their lives, he listens, nods, and says, 'I will definitely pray about that.' Then, he goes back to the outline."

A Common Complaint

Several years ago, I led a small community group, and over a 12 month period, every couple in the small group came to me complaining about the lack of transparency in the group. It was humorous that everyone in the group voiced the same concerns, but no one in the group knew what the other members were thinking or saying about each other. Fortunately, God gave us grace as the group changed into a dynamic community that was willing to delve into nearly any personal problem. In time, each individual strengthened the others in that context of loving, maturing, and caring friends. We did not get to that point by accident.

There were several things we needed to do to change into a dynamic small group. Even though all the folks were complaining privately, it was apparent they wanted something different. Thus, I had my marching orders to start setting a new tone. We were not going to be just another innocuous social gathering that shared prayer requests and snacks but a Christlike, caring community of disciple-makers. I'm not boasting about any ability I may possess. It was the grace of God that changed our group, an essential that must be present if any person, group, or situation desires change. However, you cannot dismiss that the most vital person in the group is the leader. If this person does not have the vision, intentionality, or skillset to lead well, your group will never rise higher than the person on point.

Changed By the Gospel

If you desire to be a small group leader of believers, you must know that before you can enjoy a loving, meaningful, and intrusive relationship with them, you must have an in-depth understanding and practice of the gospel in your life. Let's suppose a leader does not have a personal, practical relationship with the gospel in his life. If so, it will be nearly impossible to have a sustaining and meaningful relationship with those he wants to lead. The key idea is that you can only export what you posses. If the practical gospel is not our animating center, we will impart something other than the gospel to our immediate connections, and it will always be less than God's good intentions for us.

Perhaps it would be wise at this juncture to define how I'm using the term gospel. The gospel is Christ, His person and work. The more you understand Christ—the gospel— and the more He affects you, the more adequately you will apply the gospel to your life. The gospel (Christ) will transform you and impact your relationships in ways that nothing else can. Thus, the starting point when developing an enriching small group experience is to possess an in-depth personal and transforming relationship with the gospel. Again, you can only export what you have, and if Christ is not your animating center—the thing that drives you, then what you export will not be the gospel, and your small group experience will continue to sputter along.

Start with the Gospel

Think about the gospel (Christ) when He lived on earth. For example, Christ humbled Himself (Philippians 2:5-11) by leaving His Divine small group (Trinity) and entering into alien relationships that needed His help. Simply imitating that one data point about Christ can transform lives. Are you that intentional when you're with others? Some Christ-followers are passive in their relationships. They had rather wait, defer, and let someone else take the lead. That type of attitude is less like Christ and more like an anti-Christ. Jesus had a gospel initiative. He had an expectant assumption that people needed help, so He was always searching for opportunities to insert Himself into broken lives.

The first step to having a dynamic small group is to commit to building a vibrant personal relationship with

Christ. Do not begin with the group, but start with you and how you relate to and imitate Christ in your sphere of influence. Thus, the question you want to ask is about the effect that the gospel has had on you. You export who you are. Christ exported who He was, and your goal is to export Him to your world. The gospel is God's plan for changing His church; it is the power of God unto salvation and sanctification, and a small group of friends is an excellent place for gospel transformation (Romans 1:16). You cannot be an agent of gospel change until the gospel changes you.

Model the Gospel

Let's talk about exporting the gospel. Whatever it is that you want your small group to be like, you must model that kind of life before them. This principle is not limited to the functioning of small groups; it has as much to do with running small groups as it does with running every other part of the Christian race. For example, consider parenting. Parents must practice what they preach. How effective would it be for a parent to ask a child to confess and repent of their sin if the parent does not model and practice a similar repentance? How hypocritical for a small group leader to call the folks to holiness when he's not practicing holiness? The Bible is clear that if a parent wants a child to love God with all his heart, soul, and mind (cf. Matthew 22:36-40), that parent must own this truth by modeling what he hopes to export to the children. The call to imitate is for every person who names the name of Jesus as their Savior and Leader. Reflect on these verses.

Be imitators of me, as I am of Christ.
(1 Corinthians 11:1)

Therefore, be imitators of God as beloved children.
(Ephesians 5:1)

What you have learned and received and heard and
seen in me—practice these things, and the God of
peace will be with you.

(Philippians 4:9)

Do you want your children to have a practical dynamic
relationship with Christ? Do you want them to be honest and
transparent with God and you? Do you want them to walk in
humility and integrity? Do you want them to be accountable
to you and others? These are not the first questions that you
should ask. Start here: "How am I leading my children by
example so they can see a living illustration of the things
I want to teach them?" A small group leader should think
similarly.

The Group Jesus Led

For a moment, let's consider the small group the Savior led.
It was a thirteen-person men's group. The members had no
vision for what He wanted. They were selfish, conniving,
sinfully ambitious, critical, and easily swayed toward the
sinful opinions of others. All of them defected, and one of
them never changed, even committing suicide. I'd say that
He had a rough group of misfits. Christ was the only person
in the room who had the right vision for the small group.
Thus, you want to consider how He brought biblical shape
to His rag-tag group of misfits.

Reading the four Gospels with His leadership style in
view would be beneficial. We do know that Jesus patiently
exported His life to them. It took Him three years to whip
this bunch into shape. It would be an understatement
to say it took a lot of blood, sweat, and tears (Luke 22:42-
44). Despite the cost, Jesus patiently and carefully loved
and served His disciples as He shaped them into the most
dynamic small group in the history of the Church. In time,
all of the members (except one) of His small group became

small group leaders. As they modeled what Christ taught them, they forged other leaders, which has been the Bible's replicable plan all the way to this day.

Christ's Small Group

The message and life of Christ did not lose force after their generation. Listen to how one of the leaders of that generation spoke about himself and the work of Christian discipleship as he coached another leader.

> And what you have heard from me in the presence of many witnesses entrust to faithful men, who will be able to teach others also.
>
> (2 Timothy 2:2)

The issue of modeling the gospel is fundamental. It was essential to the Father—or else we would not have had the earthly ministry of His Son. It was necessary to the Son—or we would not have had His ministry to His small group. One of the exciting things about the four Gospels is that none of the authors wrote them as those events were unfolding. They were written after the fact. And what did they write? They wrote about what they saw Jesus do and say. Their observations were of paramount importance. They knew the necessity to deliver to us the life that the Savior modeled before them. Christ affected people by His words, actions, and deeds. If you want to see your small group go from a superficial social gathering to a Christ-centered, caring community of disciple-makers, let me urge you to begin with these two ideas:

- **KEY IDEA #1:** Before you will enjoy a loving, meaningful, and intrusive relationship with another human being, you must have an in-depth understanding, experience, and practice of the gospel (Christ) in your life.

- **KEY IDEA #2:** In whatever way you believe that someone in your small group ought to change, you become the picture of that changed life.

Call to Action

Perhaps you are not a small group leader. Do you believe this chapter is only for the leader? I trust not. All Christians are leaders. You may not be a small group leader, but God has made you an ambassador for Christ (2 Corinthians 5:20). He has called us to a leadership position. It does not matter what your sphere of influence is or even your age—if you are a believer. We never stop leading until the Lord takes us home. Thus, this chapter applies to all of us. With that perspective in mind, how would you answer these questions?

1. Are you amazed that Christ died for you? Why or why not? Describe your affection for Christ.
2. Do the realities of the gospel (Christ) practically affect your daily life? Why or why not?
3. The more you realize the depth of your darkness before Christ came into your life, the more your appreciation for the gospel will shine. What are a few specific ways God has forgiven you? How does His forgiveness motivate you to influence others? Jesus said that whoever has received much forgiveness loves much.
4. How has God's grace grown your gratitude for Him and your pity for others?
5. How does the grace of the gospel motivate you to penetrate the darkness of others to impact them for Christ?
6. Do you see yourself as a person on a gospel-centered mission when you attend your small group meetings? If not, in what specific ways will

you change? To whom will you share your plans?

7. In what ways would you like to see your small group transformed into a gospel group? Are you leading the charge? The adage is, "Practice what you preach."

8. When you think about modeling the life you want your small group to become, what fears do you have? What doubts? What specific ways do you need to change to model the life of Christ before your group?

9. Do you see the weaknesses of your group as their problem or your problem, too? Explain your answer.

5

Three Dynamic Keys

Building a close network of friends inside a local church is one of the most challenging things you'll ever do. Will you consider how you could position yourself for this kind of community—practically maturing while helping others to do similarly? Let's begin with a word cloud. As you scan the list of words, what is the common denominator that connects all of them? There are probably several excellent answers. What would you say is the one thing that ties all of these words together?

I can think of at least two things that knit these words together. This list represents our mutual commonality. We have all done some of the things on this list if not all of them. It's what it means to be in Adam. Secondly, the list represents the things that should be occurring among your closest friends, especially in your small group. If you have spent time with any small group that I have led, you would see some of these things in me, including the negative characteristics on the list. The essential point here is not whether you or I sin—for all have sinned, but what are we doing to mature in Christ? I am talking about having a context where you are free to be the most authentic and genuine person that you are currently, with the hope you're in a community of friends who love you enough to help you mature in a greater Christlikeness in the future.

Small Group Word Cloud

REPENTANCE	FORGIVENESS	HONORING	ANGER
HUMILITY	PREJUDICE	FRUSTRATION	FEAR
SELF-CONTROL	DEFERRING	FRIENDSHIP	TEXTING
GOSSIP	CRITICALNESS	FAILURE	LYING
JUSTICE	SELF-RIGHTEOUS	EMBARRASSED	UNITY
LAUGHTER	JEALOUSY	UNFORGIVENESS	PEACE
HYPOCRISY	RESTORATION	DISAPPOINTMENT	ENVY
DYSFUNCTION	CORRECTION	HANGING OUT	FUN
HURTFUL	GENTLENESS	COMPASSION	LOVE
GRUMPY	MISUNDERSTANDING	TEMPTATION	JOY

- **VULNERABLE:** Do you have a community of friends where you can live out your truest self?
- **HONEST:** Do you desire to be honest in a small group community?
- **TRANSPARENT:** Do you see the value of being in a transparent community of friends?
- **FRIENDSHIPS:** Do you perceive the danger of not doing life in a disciple-making community?

Three Men in Group

Biff has been a small group member for more than two years. From an outside-looking-in perspective, he has it all together. Of course, that is his goal, as far as how Biff wants others to perceive him. His reputation is important to him, which is why he manages it so well. What his small group does not know is that he is an angry man. His wife and kids know it. It has leaked out among a few friends, but his group does not know the real Biff. His craving for people's approval motivates him to keep this part of his life closed off from those who could love him biblically. Sadly, his desire to manage his reputation stunts his sanctification. Biff is a Christian.

Beau has been an addict since he was seventeen. He is thirty-one now. Beau has been in his small group for just over a year. He and Biff are friends. They spend many weekends together because their wives, Mable and Marge, have become close. Beau sensed that Biff was not what he claimed to be, but his thoughts were, "Shoot, who am I to judge him? I have my secret addiction." Beau's current plan is to be clean for six months to a year before he tells Marge. His thought is if he can kick the habit, he can talk about his addiction as though it was something in his past rather than a current struggle. In his twisted thinking, he wants to maintain his reputation, project humility before the group, and eventually gain some accountability just in case he falls again. His plan, like Biff's, allows him to be in control of his reputation. Rather than submitting to the foolishness and weakness of the gospel, both Biff and Beau do not want to subordinate their strengths to God's (1 Corinthians 1:18-25).

Brice enters the group. Brice is a young Christian who has not learned the ropes. Said differently, he has yet to experience the contamination from Biff's and Beau's lives. You could say Brice has not learned to embrace the value of hypocrisy or the art of deception. He is still naive enough to believe the Bible, take it at face value, and talk as though it is real. He is also a newbie to small group life. Biff and Beau have measured transparency. They reveal certain things about themselves because they want to project a facade of humility. They give the perception that they are in the small group while not indeed being part of it. Brice is amazed at their honesty and openness. From his perspective, it is radically different from the nonsense in his office. Brice is grateful for his new group.

Suppressed Transparency

Behold, you have sinned against the Lord, and be sure your sin will find you out (Numbers 32:23).

You can imagine what a surprise it was to Brice the night Biff's wife, Mable, blurted out, "I can't take it anymore. I'm leaving Biff. He's intolerable." She continued to open up, through tears, his many unknown secrets. She talked about the threats, his condemning ways, and even the physical abuse of her and the children. It was not a pretty picture. Sadly, it did not have to come out the way it did. All of us struggle with measured transparency. Just like Adam before us, our native tendency is to grab the fig leaves and cover up our shame (Genesis 3:7). In one sense, it is a form of insanity. Read the negative things in the word cloud again. It is your list. It is my list. It represents only part of our inheritance from Adam and why Jesus came to reverse the curse of our mutual fallenness.

- Why do we want to pretend those things do not belong to us?
- Why do we want to suppress our transparency?

The sad news is that the list is incomplete. Total depravity does not mean you are doing every possible evil thing you could do; it says you are capable of doing any despicable thing imaginable. Jeremiah was right (Jeremiah 17:9). Paul was right (Romans 3:10-12). Jesus was right (John 3:7). One of the blessings of being a Christian is that we have the option of finding friends who will listen and help us with our common struggles or we can resist this means of grace. Society cannot do this. They have no Jesus, no Spirit, no body of Christ, and no hope. At best, they can give you seven habits for an effective life or a "best life now" motivational speech, both of which are devoid of gospel-infused transformation.

Break the Rules

The real issue is that though we are born again, all of us continue to struggle with Adamic tendencies. We continue to drag our old "former manner of life which is corrupt through deceitful desires" around with us (Ephesians 4:22). We are eternally saved but not sanctified, which is our challenge. Our imperfections are why it is helpful to review, from time to time, what our problems are and what we can do about them. Some call it shooting the big elephant in the room, which are the things we perceive about ourselves, but we are tentative about discussing them among our friends. Here are three of those big elephants that make up every small group. If your group conquers them, you will have a dynamic small-group experience.

- Fear
- Isolation
- Sin

Fear Is Normal

Rarely will someone be like Brice; most people will hide their shame like Biff and Beau. Whenever Lucia and I have looked for a church to attend, we never put a transparent, intentional, sanctification-pursuing, small group life on our list of things we must have. We knew the church we would eventually choose would be just like us—tentative about being honest with each other. That is not an uncharitable critique but a factual statement about Adamic tendencies. All churches struggle with humble transparency because they are all made up of people like me. Rather than sinfully complaining about a church that does not pursue this type of transparency, we decided to practice openness by finding those individuals who want what we want in a sanctification community. We all are afraid of each other to varying degrees. It is weird, but it is true. Fear of man is a universal sin that affects each of us in specific and practical ways (Proverbs 29:25). Do not be surprised if your small group is anxious about being honest. One of the best things you could do is model the honesty that you desire from others.

Isolation Is Wrong

Do not settle for anything less than a group of friends who want to do intentional sanctification together. Did you know you can be humbly dissatisfied with superficiality? You do not have to be mad about it, but it is okay to be righteously dissatisfied. Ask God to give you the grace to overcome your fear of being exposed because your desire for this kind of community is stronger. Hunger for it, pray about it and ask the Lord to give it to you. Biff and Beau were deteriorating by the day with their relationship with Christ and their respective families. They were living in unexposed sin while participating in a small group that was supposedly organized to fight sin.

It is like becoming more sick while in the hospital. Biff and Beau did not understand or want to understand the value of a rich community life. Fortunately, Biff's wife had enough gumption to spill the beans. If you try to mature in your sanctification outside of a community, you will not be successful. Isolation from a small group of friends is self-defeating in that it will hinder you from following Jesus, who came to penetrate our darkness and transform us into Christlikeness. Part of the sanctification process is making disciples. Isolating from disciples is counter to the aims of the gospel (Matthew 28:19-20). It is also counter to imaging our Trinitarian (communal) Lord (Ephesians 5:1).

Sin Is Insanity

Some people reading this have hidden sins, longstanding issues, private struggles, and frustrating problems in their lives. Their spouses may not know about it, and perhaps their small group is unaware, too. Though they realize the truth of what I'm saying here, they are afraid of exposure. I appeal to you to pray. Right now. Ask the Lord to give you a grace that will enable you to talk to your small group leader about what you do not want to say aloud. You do not have to be alone, and the secrecy in your life does not have to overcome you. Today, if you hear His voice, I appeal to you not to harden your heart (Hebrews 4:7). No sin or situation has overtaken you that is uncommon to all of us Adamic creations (1 Corinthians 10:13). No sin or situation is outside of God's grace. The power of the gospel can transform you, but do not be deceived: it takes a community.

- **FEAR IS NORMAL:** Will you challenge your fears by being open with others?
- **ISOLATION IS WRONG:** Will you pursue your community while resisting isolation?
- **SIN IS INSANITY:** Will you ask your group to help you with your struggles?

Not At My Church

Two of the more common responses that I hear about non-dynamic small groups are: You do not know my church, and there is no one in my life that I can trust. Either of these may be true for you, and if so, this is where the gospel must inform your thinking. There is no human you can ultimately trust. The only person you can have as a friend is an imperfect one. Sinners will always let you down in a similar way you have disappointed others. There is risk in relationships, which is one of the stunning things about the gospel: Jesus loves us, even though we disappoint Him so often.

With that said, I know that the kind of relationships I'm talking about can be impossible to build in a local church. But you still do not have to be alone or afraid. Two of the more powerful applications of the gospel are when fear no longer controls you, and you are free to be honest about yourself while engaging others to be transparent with you. Some of our best friends do not belong to our local church. And they are the ones who bring us the best care. If you do not have this kind of relationship inside or outside your church, you're welcome to become part of our community. We are not the best option; we are not the local church, but we are available if you want it.

Call to Action

1. What will you do in response to what you have read?
2. What keeps you from being honest with your small group of friends?
3. How do you need to change? Will you change? What is your specific, detailed plan to change?

6

Loving the Difficult

How do you stay true to what you believe while not offending those who aren't willing to get on board with your perspectives? What if you have a weaker brother or sister whom you can't correct? Does the weakest link in the relationship determine how things will be? When do you take a stand for what you believe; when do you capitulate to the other person? There are always two ditches in these types of relationships. You aim to stay out of both. In one, you cater to the person because you don't want to offend them, or you could bull your way through without caring for the other person. Let me illustrate.

The Weaker Sister

Mable struggles deeply with insecurity. Three primary shaping influences have led to Mable's fearfulness. Adam has shaped her. People like her siblings, parents, and close friends have shaped her, too. The choices that she has made throughout her life have been significant shaping influences. Everyone in her Bible study knows about her fear struggles, so they typically tip-toe around her because she responds in anger whenever someone annoys her. Last year, the group leader, Marge, called on Mable during group time, asking her a personal question. While it was an appropriate question, it mortified Mable. She tightened up as fear gripped her, and a surreal tenseness came over the group.

Afterward, Mable sent Marge a nasty email, letting her know how hurt she was and that she had better not do it again. Since that time, Mable has been the de facto leader of the Bible study. No one knows that Mable has taken the role of the unspoken leader of the group except for Marge. Even Mable does not see how she leads the group. Because of Mable's insecurity and reactive anger, Marge is unwilling to delve into any personal relationship with her. The effect of Mable's sin has an even more profound impact on the group, which requires Marge to lead the group around Mable's weaknesses.

Part of Marge's abdication of leadership of the group is that she sincerely wants to care for her weaker sister. But it's also true that Marge has backed off from leading the group because she is afraid of Mable. She never knows how Mable may respond or take any offense at something. From Marge's perspective, going deep with the group is not worth the mess it might cause. So, she caters to Mable's weaknesses, and the group never goes beyond being stuck in superficiality.

Those Pink Elephants

But there is more. After Mable exploded last year, she now assumes the liberty to bring other assessments about how Marge leads the group. None of her critiques help anyone. Mable unwittingly speaks without any inhibition, coupled with a fear that anyone would challenge her, especially Marge. She hides her fear by taking the offensive. Her criticisms serve as a regular reminder that you had better not say anything out-of-line to Mable. Her critical spirit dampens the entire demeanor of the group. On the days she does not show up, the group takes on a completely different atmosphere and attitude. The difference is evident to all.

Sadly, gossip and grumbling have crept into the group. The members are wrestling with their frustration about the group's sanctification stagnation. They know that Mable is the culprit, but no one is willing to address the problem. They have chosen to uncharitably talk about what has become known as the pink elephant in the room rather than biblically dealing with it. Descending into the snare of fear is not the practical outworking of the gospel. God wants us to be redemptive in each other's lives; controlling fear does not permit you to do that. Ironically, all three players—Mable, Marge, and the group—are struggling with the same thing. They are afraid.

Who's the Leader?

At some point, Marge will have to decide whether she is going to lead her group. She can't continue to let Mable be the unstated, de facto leader. Marge has to carefully and lovingly take charge. If she does not, the whole group could unravel, and escalating unresolved conflict would ensue. One of the more unusual things about Christ was His ability to lead a complaining, insecure, and sometimes angry group of people. He never abdicated His authoritative position. He knew how to avoid the ditches of fear and self-righteousness. Sometimes, Jesus kept His mouth shut because what He had to say was not in the best interest of the group (John 16:12). At other times, He said tough things, even though He knew His words would hurt or offend His friends (John 11:14-15). There are three critical elements of His leadership style to understand when navigating this small group minefield.

- **WISDOM:** The use of wisdom means there are no cookie-cutter answers. You pneumatically respond as you bring applications of God's Word to bear on the situation at hand. You might not have a Bible verse for what you're going through, but God gives you the wisdom to know how to apply the Bible and all appropriate extrapolations from the Bible to your relationships.

- **LOVE:** The loving person carefully discerns the Spirit, so he knows how to care for each individual in unique moments. Thus, you pneumatically love others, which removes the temptation to cave to fear or judge them self-righteously. You're not better than them, and you're not afraid of them. You aim to love them.
- **FAITH:** The trusting person moves forward in faith because he knows the way the group should go. God gives him the confidence (faith) to bring the Bible to bear lovingly, even if the love stings them at the moment, and they react sinfully to the leader's care.

Weak Versus Strong

Jesus did what was best for the whole group rather than catering to the weakest member of the group. He was never unkind or unloving to the insecure person, but the weak ones did not determine His agenda. Jesus was prepping to leave our planet, but before He left, He wanted a network of reliable and equipped friends who had the competency to push His message forward globally. Though He was not about offending individuals, there were times when Jesus had to say hard things to some folks, even if it meant that some would fall away and not follow Him any longer. As hard as it is to take a stand, He knew the weak could not ultimately control His mission. Jesus would not be able to serve everybody well if He scripted His life and plans according to how the weak wanted Him to be.

This problem occurs in many of our relationships. For

example, your child becomes sick and pleads with you not to do what you should do to make him better. Maybe it is as simple as not liking the medicine. Perhaps it is a fear of a doctor or a needle in the arm. It could be something more challenging, like the fear of surgery. As a parent, you have no choice because of the love you have for God and your child. There are times when what is in the best interest of the person (or the group) means pain and suffering. If you have a weak view of love, you will not take a stand for Christ or the group. Alternatively, if you have a low view of love, you will be harsh toward others.

Gospel-Motivated Care

Remember the gospel? It pleased the Father to bruise His Son because of the greater good (Isaiah 53:10). God so loved the world that He did the difficult and painful things to His chosen beloved (John 3:16). If fear controls any of us, it will be impossible to respond to God in obedience with a robust application of love. These decisions are hard to make, but you have to make them carefully, prayerfully, and with wise counsel. A Bible study or small group leader needs to get the counsel of an elder of oversight or pastor. Someone up the chain needs to speak into this situation with Mable. If you don't have such a person, you can always reach out to us. We're not the best answer; we are not the local church, but it can be a practical safety net for now.

Maybe someone in the group besides Marge can come alongside Mable to serve her. The goal would be to restore her to God and her group. Mable cannot run the group because of her fears. Marge needs to repent of her fear of man (Proverbs 29:25). She must take control of the group for the glory of God. The group must repent of any gossip about Mable while resisting the temptation to succumb to speech that does not build up each other (Ephesians 4:29). In the best-case scenario, Marge, Mable, and the group will repent to God for their unique fear of man sins. Should Marge become the de facto leader, and Mable and the group follow, they will become a sanctification group. Of course, it is possible that Mable does not repent and may leave the group. Marge cannot become a mini-messiah. She must entrust these things to the Lord, caring more about His opinion of her than Mable's.

> When the young man heard this, he went away sorrowful, for he had great possessions.
> (Matthew 19:22)

Call to Action

1. Which temptation is more natural for you: to back off because of fear or jump in impulsively with harshness?
2. What does your temptation reveal about your relationship with God? How do you need to change so you can be a better friend practically?
3. Is there someone who controls your life other than God? Why do you give them control?
4. Are you more apt to talk critically about that person who controls you or strategically and redemptively plan about how you can cooperate with the Lord in restoring the caught person (Galatians 6:1-2)?
5. Are you the weak person who manipulates others because of your insecurity? Will you find help today so you're not controlling others and impeding the work of God in your life, as well as theirs?
6. Do you know how to say the hard things with love? Are you willing to say those things even if you lose the relationship? Perhaps it would be great if you studied the four Gospels where Jesus responded in ways that created sinful reactions from others.

7

Let's Get Practical

Building a robust small group of Christlike disciple-makers takes work. One of the most challenging responsibilities in the church is that of the small group leader. They are like pastors on the ground. Though they are not typically pastors, they function as ad hoc shepherds because they are shepherding the flock in some of the most crucial areas of Christians' lives. Thus, knowing how to build and sustain a small group is paramount. This chapter will not answer all the questions a small group leader might have, but I want to share a few ideas, and I will do that by responding to a letter a friend wrote me about their experience and aspirations for a small group.

> We have visited several churches that have small groups. Each has a form to fill out to express your interest, and they ask you to provide your age group. Every church I've ever been to wants small groups according to age. Am I the only one who is confused by this? What is the effectiveness of this method? I'm not sure if they do this because it is an easy way to group people or because it is the best way. Maybe I am not seeing this correctly, and someone could enlighten me. My husband and I attended a small group where members were of various ages and stages of life. There were grandparents,

empty nesters, high schoolers' parents, and small children's parents.

In this small group, we experienced tremendous growth, were spiritually challenged, and had accountability. I enjoyed learning from older, wiser Christians who could say, "We went through that too, and this is how we made it." If people are all the same age, they can share and relate to their issues, but few would have answers or wisdom about how to navigate those challenges or offering hope. (For the record, I get keeping singles and married folks separate, but other than that, I'm at a loss.) So my question remains: why do churches want to divide people into small groups according to their age?

– Small Group Member

Preliminary Thoughts

The Bible does not stipulate how to operate a small group. Thus, each church determines how they want to run theirs, which varies from church to church. Your first course of action is to talk to the leaders to find out why they have small groups the way they do. There is a purpose and freedom in play here since the Bible does not stipulate, so your preference is not out-of-line with God's Word, but you want to recognize that each church has reasons for doing what they do. Our role as church members is to obey and support our leaders while engaging the contexts they provide to serve each other (Hebrews 13:17). Each believer or family must determine what they want while always supporting the local church on secondary issues. Though no church can meet every preference of every member, we must always seek to intentionally spur one another on to love and good works while using the means of grace the local church provides.

> And let us consider how to stir up one another to love
> and good works, not neglecting to meet together, as
> is the habit of some, but encouraging one another,
> and all the more as you see the Day drawing near.
> (Hebrews 10:24-25)

Realizing that we're talking about preferences here and not biblical mandates is vital. I will share with you my preference for small groups, which are mixed groups of all ages. The education system and Sunday school are two of the few contexts in the world that are uni-generational. Virtually every other context where people come together is multi-generational, e.g., family, work, hobbies, fitness centers, shopping, church, etc. In all of these contexts, nobody thinks twice about the multi-generational makeup of these gatherings. Thus, a small group with mixed generations looks like the rest of our lives. However, in academic learning environments and Sunday school, there is an emphasis on uni-generational contexts due to everyone learning in a structured and sequenced manner. For example, you would not want a first-grader in a sixth-grade classroom. But what better equipping environment can you create than a mixed-generational small group in a local church that trains the saints to live well in all the other mixed-generation contexts of their lives?

Mixed Positives

People will naturally gravitate to their preferred kind, i.e., young kids will seek to play with kids their age. Married couples enjoy other married couples. There is nothing wrong with these types of connections. People pursuing like-minded people is a good thing. Typically, you do not have to push for kind-to-kind connections because we do it naturally. We find someone we click with, and we build relationships with them. However, if you want something more than peer-to-peer, like-minded interactions, you'll have to create it intentionally. Just as there are benefits to kind-to-kind relationships, there are many blessings that come from mixed groups. Let me share a few examples.

- Mixed groups position us to engage all kinds of people, not just those we are naturally drawn. We learn from those who are different from us because their varied experiences are not ours.
- Mixed groups prepare Christians for different types of people and problems. You've heard of living in an echo chamber, right? In a mixed group, the chances of being stretched beyond your comfort zone are strong.
- Mixed groups train people to be more effective disciple-makers because you learn from those who are living a different experience. How marvelous would it be for young couples to have empty-nesters in their group?
- Mixed groups provide younger children safe places to interact with adults. It is better for them to learn how to interact with adults long before they become one.
- Young people can learn from role models, whether older singles or married couples.
- Singles can learn from married couples, which is a huge plus since most of them will spend their lives married. For example, a lot of Titus 2 activity could happen in a small group context.
- Middle-aged couples can learn how to serve those younger than them by stepping into their stories. Instead of talking about "how things used to be," they can learn how things are today. These older saints can also pursue cultural relevance while maximizing their cultural engagement.
- Of course, these older people can offer wisdom

to anyone in the group because they are the least myopic demographic. Experience does come with age, and when you have an older, mature, wise saint in the room that the younger generations can learn from, it is sanctification gold.

Small Group Methodology

If you want a dynamic small group experience, you must do more than have a mixed group of individuals from various backgrounds and ages. You should also have an intentional plan to build into the small group members' lives. I talked about this in a prior chapter, but I want to revisit it here because some may think that you only need a small group meeting to do life well together. In all my years of leading a small group, most of the sanctification has happened outside of the small group meeting. It occurs in these smaller groups where a person is more willing to be vulnerable, transparent, and honest about the things that are critical to them. The least number of people in the room is your best chance to get folks to open up about their deepest concerns. The graphic explains the deliberate strategy my wife and I used when we led small groups.

Corporate meetings provide at least fifty-two contact points in each other's lives during the year. If you have more corporate meetings, i.e., Sunday evening, you double these opportunities to connect with each other. One of the goals is to build relational bridges with the members of your group. You don't want to disciple someone you hardly know. The corporate meeting is a great context for building that relational bridge. A lot of small talk can lead to the deep conversations you long for, so you take advantage of these short rendezvous on Sunday morning, in addition to the teaching and singing.

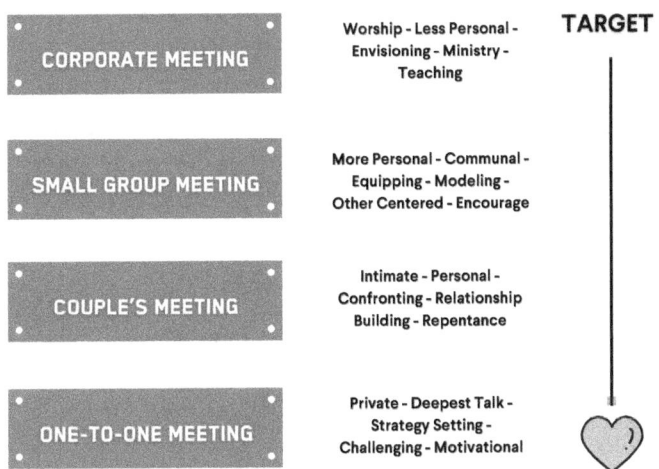

CORPORATE MEETING	Worship - Less Personal - Envisioning - Ministry - Teaching	**TARGET**
SMALL GROUP MEETING	More Personal - Communal - Equipping - Modeling - Other Centered - Encourage	
COUPLE'S MEETING	Intimate - Personal - Confronting - Relationship Building - Repentance	
ONE-TO-ONE MEETING	Private - Deepest Talk - Strategy Setting - Challenging - Motivational	

Small group meetings have fewer people, which is conducive to more intimate conversations. With fifty-two contact points under your belt on Sunday morning, you can intentionally and incrementally go deeper in a small group setting where you have more time and fewer distractions to talk about more meaningful things. The keyword is intentionality. If you're not intentional about connecting at the corporate or small group meetings, then redemptive transformation will not move forward.

Couple-to-couple (or leader-to-singles) meetings increase the possibility of transparency exponentially. Some people will never say what they want to say in a small group, but they might open up in the privacy of your home, where you're doing hospitality for the express purpose of biblical koinonia. Also, some things should never be said in a small group. In many cases, there is a transient aspect to small groups, where new folks are coming and going, especially during the holidays, for example. Not knowing each of the members in the group well enough to open up precludes the more intimate conversations.

Guy-to-guy meetings are the most intimate of all. When two men or two women come together to do life over coffee, there are no distractions and few inhibitions if the leader has taken advantage of the other contexts for small group development. These final two contexts are where most of the transformation has happened in my small groups. The guy-to-guy meetings are also an excellent time to envision a potential leader about how to take initiative in the larger group. You want him to step up and lead.

The Church Culture

Suppose the church's culture lacks a robust, transparent, vulnerable, honest, courageous, charitable, authentic gospel DNA, as I have been outlining in this book. In that case, it will not be easy to build a sanctification group within that local body. These values do not work well in a subset (small group) of the local church if the larger body is not embracing these ideas. However, in a church that values relationships, as I have outlined, it will be easier for the shepherds on the ground to lead their small groups into deeper, transformative relationships. Of course, all this begins with the leadership and their spouses. If the leaders and spouses are not living in and benefiting from biblical koinonia, the small group leaders can't learn, live, and export it to the greater church body.

Call to Action

1. Which type of group do you prefer, and why do you like it? What are the upsides to your preference? What are the downsides?
2. In what ways can a mixed small group experience supplement your parenting objectives? Suppose you have young children. How many ways could they benefit from being around adults weekly in a small group context?
3. Why is intentionality essential to have a dynamic small group experience? What would happen if the leader was not intentional about these strategies? What if the small group members were not intentional? What would you do to change their perspectives?
4. How would you describe your church culture relating to having a robust, intentional, vulnerable, courageous, transparent, and honest desire to live together in a community? Be honest. Do you believe a small group experience that I have described here would work in the larger culture of your church? Why did you answer that way?
5. If you desire this kind of small group experience, what are the first steps you need to take to develop this kind of group in your church? Will you share your thoughts with someone you believe would be on board with your plan?

8

A Guide for Leaders

Small groups can be a vital part of any church's discipleship initiatives and aspirations. These groups provide a context where believers can grow in Christ, care for one another, and deepen their faith in a personal, practical, and relational way. It is one way the leaders of the church can equip the saints to do the work of the ministry. Dynamic small groups are not the only way to do church life, but providing robust and thriving contexts for practical one-anothering has the potential to have a generational impact on the local church.

> And he gave the apostles, the prophets, the evangelists, the shepherds and teachers, to equip the saints for the work of ministry, for building up the body of Christ, until we all attain to the unity of the faith and of the knowledge of the Son of God, to mature manhood, to the measure of the stature of the fullness of Christ, so that we may no longer be children, tossed to and fro by the waves and carried about by every wind of doctrine, by human cunning, by craftiness in deceitful schemes. Rather, speaking the truth in love, we are to grow up in every way

into him who is the head, into Christ, from whom the whole body, joined and held together by every joint with which it is equipped, when each part is working properly, makes the body grow so that it builds itself up in love.

(Ephesians 4:11-16)

This chapter will cover a few key principles for leading an effective small group and answer common questions such as how to foster openness, balance participation, and select sound study material.

The Leader

If you've ever been part of a small group that just clicks— where people are real, conversations go deep, and the relationships mature—you know how powerful that kind of community can be. But that kind of environment doesn't happen by accident. It takes intentional leadership, a heart for discipleship, and a commitment to shepherding people toward Christ. As a small group leader, you're not just a discussion facilitator. You're creating a space where people can encounter God, wrestle with truth, and build genuine relationships. Your role is both practical and spiritual.

One of the distinctions the church leadership will have to make is the difference between a leader and a facilitator. Most small group leaders are not leaders but appointed church members who facilitate a group. They may host the group and lead the prepared discussion, which is a vital aspect of thriving small groups. However, a genuine leader can decouple from a script or three-point outline. A small group leader is beholding to the Word of God and Spirit of God, living pneumatically, reading the room, and always ready to deviate on any given evening to do on-the-spot, unscripted soul care. The pneumatos (walking in the Spirit) matters to him, and he's discerning, willing, and able to be an effective disciple-maker. Too often, the role of a small group leader is given to someone who is sincere, but a facilitator. Should he see a sanctification problem with someone in the group, he will do three things at best:

- Give them a passage from God's Word.
- Pray for them.
- Let a pastor know that one of his small group members has a sanctification problem.

Brothers, if anyone is caught in any transgression, you who are spiritual should restore him in a spirit of gentleness. Keep watch on yourself, lest you too be tempted. Bear one another's burdens, and so fulfill the law of Christ. For if anyone thinks he is something, when he is nothing, he deceives himself.
(Galatians 6:1-3)

Though these things are great and prerequisite, they are not enough for a small group leader—if it's a sanctification group. A leader leads folks to Christ. He knows how to do soul care. He has the competency to bring God's Word to bear on real-life problems. He does not see himself as a placeholder to fill a spot—to merely facilitate a meeting. He brings a gospel edge—the sword of God's Word—to the soul of someone who needs restoration (Hebrews 4:11-12). In Galatians 6:1-3, the word *restore* means to mend, as in mending a broken net (Mark 1:19). A small group leader can see what is broken and bring restorative care to the person. A small group facilitator prefers to stay on script. If there are sanctification problems, he will pass them along to a competent disciple-maker. Knowing the difference between a small group leader and a facilitator is essential. Not understanding these key differences may lead to confusion, misplaced expectations, and grumbling among the saints.

The Environment

If people don't feel safe, they won't open up. It's that simple. Many Christians struggle with being real about their lives, especially in a church setting where there's pressure to appear like we have it all together. But genuine change happens in a place of honesty, not pretense. Of course, you have the added complexity of a transient small group with new people coming in or visiting. When Mable brings her mother to the small group meeting during the holidays, the entire vibe of the group changes, as it should. With Mable's mother visiting the group, you don't want Bert blurting out his latest fight with Marge. Mable does not have the context or concerns of the other folks in the group. Thus, a small group leader will have to be discerning with how he creates a transparent small group.

Of course, it begins with the leader and his wife—if he is married. People will only be as open as their leader. If they sense that you're guarded, they'll follow suit. But if you're willing to share your struggles, they'll see that this is a space where honesty and transparency are welcomed. You want to be appropriate, of course; a fool will reveal his entire mind, so discretion is vital. Thus, you want to lead by being honest and transparent about your life, specifically your struggles. You want to ensure your wife agrees with you—you're on the same page. The last thing you want to do is surprise her in the middle of group night with some dark secret about your life. Paul sets the example for this type of leadership in 1 Corinthians 11:1—"Be imitators of me, as I am of Christ." He didn't pretend to have it all figured out. He openly shared his weaknesses, his battles, and the ways God was working in him. That's the kind of leadership that invites people to be real. Perhaps you would lead by saying:

- "Here's an area where I struggle."
- "This is how God is convicting me."
- "I don't have all the answers, but I'm growing."

When you lead this way, others will follow, albeit probably not the first night you begin opening up about your life. Get to know each other first. Vulnerability doesn't happen overnight. Many people have been hurt in past church experiences or personal relationships, and it may take months—or even years—before they open up. One woman in our group took 18 months before she finally shared the most painful event of her life. Why? Because she was watching, waiting to see if this was truly a safe place. However, she did not open up in our small group meeting but in our couple's meeting. She needed fewer people around to reveal her most significant disappointment. She trusted us but did not fully trust the group, and she was also unsure if it was appropriate to share what she wanted to say in the larger small group setting. Fortunately, she had another context with her group to open up about an event that happened decades prior. The burden she released that night was palpable. Here are a few keys to instilling this kind of trust in your small group.

- **CONSISTENCY:** Show up, be dependable, and follow through on commitments. God is with us, and you want to imitate Him. We lead by being present, ready, and willing to serve.
- **CARE:** Listen actively, ask good questions, and respond with love. When they share, give them eye contact, show them you care, and ask insightful questions that expand on their concerns.
- **CONFIDENTIALITY:** One of our mantras is, "What's shared in the group stays in the group." When people see that you are trustworthy, they will begin to open up. Of course, there are limitations since you do

not know what someone might say. There are a few things you must not keep confidential.

- **CASUAL CONVERSATION:** We like to say that "small talk leads to deep talk." Don't despise small talk. Chit-chatting with a friend provides the material for a fortified relational bridge that you will need when the day comes to convey heavyweight and potentially confrontational truth to them. Don't underestimate the power of casual conversation. Small talk about jobs, kids, hobbies, or even last night's game may seem unimportant, but it lays the groundwork for deeper discussions. Relationships grow in everyday moments. When people enjoy being together, they're more likely to be honest when things get tough. Make time for lighthearted conversations. Those moments of laughter and connection are what make people feel at home in your group.

The Expectations

Every small group has a mix of personalities—some people love to talk, while others stay quiet. A good leader ensures that everyone has a voice. You want to ensure that everyone in the group understands the purpose and the practice of the group. Don't assume they will know how to participate in your small group. Just because Biff and Mable have been in a small group for twenty years, it was not your small group. It is best to set the tone at the onset of your initial small group meeting. If you have been meeting for a while and want to make a change of direction, you can do that by stating something like the following:

> Our goal is to help one another grow in Christ by being open about our struggles and encouraging each other. We are a sanctification group, which means we are here to spur one another on to love

and good works as we learn in (Hebrews 10:24-25).
We want everyone to have a voice; part of how we
do this is listening well and respecting each other's
contributions.

This simple statement helps those who tend to dominate the conversation to be mindful of others while reassuring the quieter members that their input matters. However, everyone will not get the message. Babbling Bart will not automatically become a quieter. It is not who he has been all his life. Mumbling Mable will not become talkative either. Your goal is to set the expectation and then refer back to it again and again until it is the group's DNA to speak appropriately and listen effectively. You'll also have those who talk in circles, avoiding what's really going on. Others vent about surface-level frustrations but never address the deeper issue. As a leader, listen beneath the words. Luke 6:45 says, "Out of the abundance of the heart, the mouth speaks." What people say often reveals their more acute and deeper struggles. For example, if a woman complains about her husband, the real issue might also be disappointment, bitterness, and unforgiveness. Instead of just nodding along, ask:

- "How did you respond to that?"
- "Have you taken this to the Lord? What was the result?"
- "How do you believe God is using this in your life?"

This astute shift brings focus while practically moving the conversation from venting to growth in Christ. Another example is if someone dominates the conversation. Don't ignore it—gently guide the discussion back to balance by using directive questions: "John, what are your thoughts on this?" Or, "That's a great insight—let's hear from someone else." If you have a co-leader, they can step in and redirect.

I call them "ringers," folks who understand what I want to accomplish, and they take part of the burden from me by inserting themselves in order to get the flow of the group back on track. My wife is one of my ringers, and I seek to develop more people in the group by identifying those who are further along the path in their sanctification. Part of their development is teaching the principles from this book. Everyone will not be at the same place, so you want to identify potential leaders and begin developing them.

The Materials

Not all Christian books and Bible studies are helpful. Some are full of personal opinions rather than biblical truth. Though it should go without saying it, I will say it anyway: a small group should never use material that contradicts Scripture. If your church provides or permits recommended studies, use those. Otherwise, seek input from church leadership before choosing a book, resource, or study. Some groups go through Christian books, while others discuss their church's sermons. Both have benefits.

Books provide structure but can lead to discussing someone else's story rather than personal application. I have never gone through a book with anyone because my preference is to talk to them about themselves instead of discussing subjects or subject matter from a book. I'd rather not look at a third party when I have primary source material in the person sitting across from me. It's too easy to talk about "Biff and Mable" from [this great book] and not talk about ourselves. However, this strategy is a leadership decision, and some small group leaders prefer the template of a book to help guide them along, which is more of a facilitator unless the leader can "go off script" when someone in the group needs soul care.

Sermon-based studies keep discussions grounded in Scripture and encourage members to apply the Sunday message. For our groups, we have found that sermon-based interactions are the most effective because they keep the focus on God's Word rather than personal opinions. Also, we are applying what the pastor taught us on Sunday morning. Nobody knows the church better than the lead pastor. Nobody has spent more time constructing material for the church than the person who prepared and preached Sunday's sermon. It seems prudent to me to follow his lead by taking all his prep and preaching and working hard to practicalize it in our small group. Rather than listening to the sermon and delving into something else, for me, it is a matter of honoring his labor by taking his hard work and working it out in our small group. This perspective also creates a better continuity between orthodoxy (the preached Word) and orthopraxy (the practicalized Word).

The Community

A thriving small group isn't just about the weekly small group meeting. True discipleship happens in everyday life. When people live life together, they naturally grow in Christ together. One of your goals is to encourage your group members to meet beyond the stated group night. Some of the deepest discipleship happens in private conversations. Here are a few things you want to encourage them to do:

- Get together for coffee or meals.
- Support each other in hard times.
- Celebrate birthdays, promotions, and life events.
- Encourage one-to-one and couple-to-couple meetings.
- Men meeting with men for encouragement and accountability.
- Women meeting with women for prayer and growth.

Leading a small group isn't easy. Small group leaders are pastors on the ground or shepherds in the field. They may not carry the title of pastor, but their work is very much pastoral. It requires patience, intentionality, and a humble willingness to serve. But the reward? Seeing the power of the gospel transform lives. It is also a tremendous reward and relief to your pastors when you are equipped to do the work of ministry. The amount of soul care that can happen within small groups is inestimable, and it becomes the sanctification lifeblood of any local church. A small group leader's faithfulness will bear fruit—maybe not overnight, but in God's perfect timing. Keep pressing on, and trust that He is working through you.

Call to Action

1. What is the difference between a small group leader and a small group facilitator?
2. Why is it essential to lead others with your honesty and transparency?
3. Why is it vital to establish a vision and purpose for the group and revisit it from time to time?
4. What does it mean to go off-script, to walk in the Spirit?
5. What are the advantages of book studies? What about about Sunday's sermon?
6. Why is it vital to meet together outside of the regular small group meeting?

Conclusion

Where do you begin when it comes to establishing and building friendships? May I suggest that you start with an uber-honesty with God? Building relationally with others should always begin with the Lord. Start by telling Him what He already knows about you. If you are married, at some point, you want to bring your spouse into these intimate and vulnerable moments with the Lord. Most of us have a secret world of shame, hurt, pain, and dread. With baby steps, we must begin sharing our vulnerable selves with those we trust.

When Pursuing Others

Next, you begin a search for like-minded believers who want to go to this level with you. Assuredly, this will be like looking for the proverbial needle in a haystack, but those people are out there. Ask God to help you find them and then draw them to you. God has been kind to Lucia and me by giving us a small group of believers with whom we can share our most intimate struggles, flaws, sins, arguments, and disappointments. Here are three pointers that have served us well.

- **BE PREPARED:** Don't assume others will have your vision for or your understanding of true biblical fellowship, also called koinonia. Many Christians have yet to experience grace-based transparent relationships. Their experience has been more along the lines of judgment and alienation.

- **BE PATIENT:** Guard your heart from self-righteously judging others who are not willing to pursue this kind of relationship with you. There are good reasons they are unwilling to go there with you. If you can, help them get there. You want to understand their experience. And, by all means, lead by example. It is the kindness of God that leads to repentance (Romans 2:4).

- **BE PROACTIVE:** If you want this kind of fellowship in your life, you'll have to make it happen purposefully. It will not happen on its own. People do not, as a general rule, seek to close the gap between who they know themselves to be and the person they present to the general public.

Fellowship Questions

The following is a list of questions that Lucia and I use to get closer to God and each other. It has taken years to reach this place of triune spiritual intimacy—God, husband, and wife—but it was well worth the work and process. These questions are perfect for any two or more Christians. Perhaps while doing life over coffee with a friend, you might add to our list.

1. Will you help me in this [specific area] of temptation in my life?
2. What is God doing in your life? Be specific, practical, and real with your answer.
3. How is the grace of God working in a particular area of sin? How is He helping you to overcome this issue?
4. What is a specific area in which you continue to struggle?

5. What have you read or heard lately that is helping you in your sanctification?
6. How can I serve you in a specific area of sanctification in your life?
7. What are some ways in which you lead others and help them grow in their relationship with God?

You're welcome to share these questions in your small group, perhaps incorporating them as part of how you typically speak with each other. Initially, it will feel a bit mechanical or wooden if these types of questions are new to you. However, with much practice, it will become your common language, and you'll never return to your former manner of life.

Thank you for reading my book. I trust it has inspired you to build deeply with others. Perhaps the Lord would use this resource in your small group and church. Doing life together does not happen passively, automatically, or even with good intentions. It takes determination, effort, a few failures, and perseverance. The good news is that there is grace for our relationships, and as we appropriate it to our lives, we can experience a dynamic life with others.

Rick

About the Author

 Rick Thomas launched the Life Over Coffee global training network in 2008 to bring hope and help for you and others by creating resources that spark conversations for transformation. His primary responsibilities are resource creation and leadership development, which he does through speaking, writing, podcasting, and educating. In 1990 he earned a BA in Theology and, in 1991, a BS in Education. In 1993, he received his ordination into Christian ministry, and in 2000, he graduated with an MA in Counseling from The Master's University. In 2006, he was recognized as a Fellow of the Association of Certified Biblical Counselors (ACBC).

Other Books Available from
Life Over Coffee

Boasting in Weakness
Centering Your Marriage on Christ
Communication
Complete Marriage
Don't Apologize
Exchange the Truth for a Lie
Help My Marriage Has Grown Cold
Identity Crisis
Local Church
Loving Me
Mad
Marriage Devotion We Are One
Politics and Culture
Parenting Devotion from Zero to Adulthood
Sex, Temptation, and Modesty
Storm Hurler
The Cyber Effect
The Talk
Wives Leading
You Decide